the SCIENCE *libr*

INVENTIONS

D0825830

the SCIENCE *library*

INVENTIONS

Barbara Taylor
Consultant: John Farndon

Miles Kelly
PUBLISHING

First published in 2004 by Miles Kelly Publishing Ltd
Bardfield Centre Great Bardfield Essex CM7 4SL

Copyright © 2004 Miles Kelly Publishing Ltd

This edition printed in 2008

2 4 6 8 10 9 7 5 3

All rights reserved. No part of this publication may be reproduced, stored in a retrieval system, or transmitted by any means, electronic, photocopying, recording or otherwise, without the prior permission of the copyright holder.

British Library Cataloguing-in-Publication Data
A catalogue record for this book is available from the British Library

Editorial Director Belinda Gallagher

Art Director Jo Brewer

Editor Jenni Rainford

Editorial Assistant Chloe Schroeter

Cover Design Simon Lee

Design Concept Debbie Meekcoms

Design Stonecastle Graphics

Consultant John Farndon

Indexer Hilary Bird

Reprographics Stephan Davis, Ian Paulyn

Production Manager Elizabeth Brunwin

ISBN 978-1-84236-992-0

Printed in China

www.mileskelly.net
info@mileskelly.net

www.factsforprojects.com

Third-party website addresses are provided by Miles Kelly Publishing
in good faith and for information only, and are suitable and accurate at the time of going to press.
Miles Kelly Publishing Ltd disclaims any responsibility for the material contained therein.

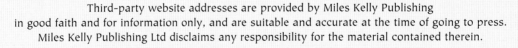

Contents

How to use this book

INVENTIONS is packed with information, colour photos, diagrams, illustrations and features to help you learn more about science. Do you know who invented the microwave or when the wheel was first used? Did you know that the ancient Egyptians wore shoes or that people may soon be able to fly without an aeroplane? Enter the fascinating world of science and learn about why things happen, where things come from and how things work. Find out how to use this book and start your journey of scientific discovery.

It's a fact
Key statistics and extra facts on each subject provide additional information.

Main text
Each page begins with an introduction to the different subject areas.

The grid
The pages have a background grid. Pictures and captions sit on the grid and have unique co-ordinates. By using the grid references, you can move from page to page and find out more about related topics.

Keeping in touch

UNTIL PEOPLE learned to write they were only able to communicate when speaking face to face. Information was passed verbally through the generations, often through story-telling. About 5000 years ago the Sumerians and ancient Egyptians invented writing. Then about 4000 years later, the Chinese invented printing by hand. The mechanical printing press was invented about 500 years ago in Europe by Johannes Gutenberg. Other communication methods, such as Braille and Morse code, were invented in the 1800s. Today e-mails, telephones and fax machines connect people all over the world, and because of the Internet, information is easier to access than ever before.

● **IT'S A FACT**
• In 1455, the first book printed by Gutenberg was the Bible.
• Sign language for the deaf was invented in 1620 by J.P. Bonnet, a tutor at the Spanish court.

◄ *The printing press enabled newspapers and books to be read by more people.*

● **Clues to the past**
The ancient Egyptians used written pictures and symbols, called hieroglyphics, instead of words. They used these hieroglyphics for 3500 years until about AD 400 when Greek became their written language. The Rosetta Stone, discovered in 1799, written in both hieroglyphics and Greek, provided the key to translating hieroglyphics.

● **Printing**
Before printing was invented, books were copied by hand. Invented in China before AD 868, 'letterpress' printing used letters and pictures carved from blocks of wood, clay or ivory, which were covered with ink so that when paper was pressed on them they printed the raised carving. Peking blacksmith Pi-Sheng invented movable type (individual letters on reusable blocks). In 1436 German Johannes Gutenberg invented typecasting, which made large amounts of movable type quickly and cheaply. In 1886, the linotype machine automatically cast complete lines of type from molten metal. Today, computers are used to input and print type and images.

➤➤ **Read further ▸** pg11 (b33)

➤➤ **Read further ▸ picture writing** pg9 (b22)

◄ *Each hieroglyph (symbol or picture) represented an object or a sound. In total, there were about 700 different hieroglyphs.*

COMMUNICAT

Invention	Year first
Writing	about 3.
Paper	AD 105
Numbers 0 to 9	about
Mechanical clock	1000s
Printing press	1400

Optical fibres carry information about 30 per cent faster than the electrical signals carried by copper 1

1 2 3 4 5 6 7 8 9 10 11 12 13 14 15 16

Main image
Each topic is clearly illustrated. Some images are labelled, providing further information.

Photos and artworks
Illustrations and photographs accompany each caption. Diagrams are labelled to give more detailed scientific facts and information.

a b c d e f g h i j k l m n o p q r s t u v w

Dot writing
In 1829, Frenchman Louis Braille invented a six-dot coded system of raised dots that could be used by the blind to read. Louis Braille was accidentally blinded at the age of three. When he was ten, he was shown a way of writing messages with raised dots, designed for soldiers to use at night. Braille simplified it so it was easier to read with the fingertips. Braille is still used worldwide today.

▼ Braille is made up of different patterns of six dots, each pattern representing a letter and some short words such as 'the'.

Read further > symbols
▶▶ pg9 (b22)

Dots and dashes
In 1838 Samuel Morse and Alfred Vail stopped and started an electric current along wires (or telegraphs) to communicate. Named Morse code, the short (on) bursts were the dots, and the longer (off) bursts were the dashes. In 1844, the first telegraph line opened between Baltimore and Washington, DC, enabling messages that would normally take weeks by post, to be sent instantly. Within 30 years, telegraphs covered the globe. Morse code is still used by the Navy today.

Long and short bleeps tapped into telegraph machine

Electric current

Message travels along telegraph wires to recipient

▲ As an electric current running along a wire is stopped and started, the on and off bursts form coded messages.

Read further > radio
▶▶ pg24 (q11)

Cross-references
Attached to captions and pictures are cross-references that use the unique co-ordinates grid system. These lead you to related subjects within the book.

The Internet
The Internet is a worldwide network of computers. Developed in the 1970s by American computer scientist Vinton Cerf and American engineer Robert Kahn, it connects, using phone lines, local networks of computers to special computers called gateways. Cerf and Kahn defined the Internet Protocol – the software that controls the Internet. Then, in 1989, English computer scientist Tim Berners-Lee invented the World Wide Web to share information over the Internet. At the beginning of the 21st century, more than 25 million computers were linked to the Internet, and this number continues to rise.

▶ Internet phones allow people to 'surf' (browse) the Internet from all over the world.

Read further > computers
▶▶ pg25 (h22)

Check it out!
Find out more by surfing the Internet.

Telephones old and new
Telephones were invented by Scottish-born American Alexander Graham Bell in 1876. Bell discovered how to change sound vibrations in the human voice into electrical signals, which he sent along wires to a receiver. Today, pulses of light send telephone calls down fibre optic cables, and electrical signals are sent along copper cables. The word 'telephone' comes from the Greek words for 'far' and 'sound'.

◀ Mobile phones, invented in the 1980s, send digital radio signals to base stations, which send the signal around a network until it reaches the right phone.

Read further > satellites
▶▶ pg33 (c30)

To scale
1 square across = 6 cm

Check it out!
• http://www.bbc.co.uk/arts/books/historyofbooks
• http://www.worldalmanacfor kids.com/explore/inventions.html

20 cm across
Bell's first telephone

20 21 22 23 24 25 26 27 28 29 30 31 32 33 34 35 36 37 38 39

Amazing facts
Look out for facts that run along the bottom of each page.

To scale
This feature uses the grid to show comparative size of different objects. You can easily compare and see exactly how small or large things are.

Early inventions

PEOPLE HAVE been inventing things for about 2.5 million years to make their lives easier and more comfortable. Writing was not invented until about 5000 years ago, so the origins of the earliest inventions were not written down. We only know about them from archaeological discoveries. The first inventions were stone tools and weapons made by early hunters and gatherers. Later, they carved needles from bones to sew clothes for warmth. When people began to settle in one place about 10,000 years ago, they invented wheels, ploughs and irrigation devices to water their crops. They made jars and pots to store food, and better weapons to defend their settlements. However, labour-saving devices were not developed, possibly because work was often carried out by slaves.

IT'S A FACT

• The ancient Egyptians invented locks about 4000 years ago. The same principle is still used in some parts of Egypt today.

• The ancient Egyptians used saws to cut wood and stone 6000 years ago. Saw marks can be seen on the stones of the pyramids.

• About 5000 years ago, ancient Egyptians pressed peeled papyrus reeds with linen, to make paper.

Digging made easy

The earliest known picture of a plough dates from about 5500 years ago in the ancient city of Ur (present-day Iraq). The first plough was wooden and developed from simple digging sticks used to make holes for planting seeds. Its wedge-like blade made long furrows in the soil as it moved forward. After the discovery of iron about 2500 years ago, farmers used iron blades on their ploughs, which were stronger than wooden blades and cut deeper into the soil. The first all-iron plough was invented in 1785 by Robert Ransome in Britain.

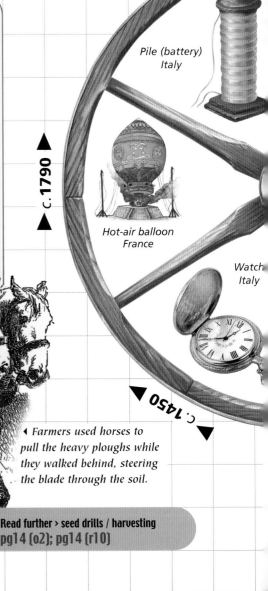

▼ c. 1800
Pile (battery) Italy

c. 1790

Hot-air balloon France

Watch Italy

c. 1450

◄ Farmers used horses to pull the heavy ploughs while they walked behind, steering the blade through the soil.

▶▶ Read further > seed drills / harvesting
pg14 (o2); pg14 (r10)

The letters J, V, and W in the written alphabet were not invented until the Middle Ages, c. 1100 to 1500

1   2   3   4   5   6   7   8   9   10   11   12   13   14   15   16   17   18   19

a
b
c
d
e
f
g

Reading the past

We know about ancient civilizations, such as those of the Sumerians (who lived in part of modern Iraq) and the Egyptians because of the picture writing they left behind. About 5250 years ago the Sumerians were the first people to write down their language properly, using pictures to represent words. They developed this into wedge-shaped signs on clay tablets called cuneiform writing (cuneiform means wedge-shaped). The Egyptians developed a form of picture writing known as hieroglyphics (see pg26 [t6]).

▶▶ **Read further › picture writing**
pg18 (m2); pg26 (m2)

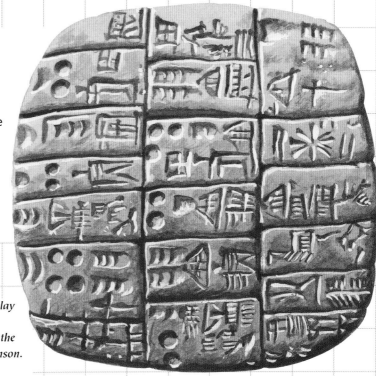

▶ *The cuneiform writing on clay tablets, dating from the 6th century BC, was translated in the 19th century by Henry Rawlinson.*

h
i
j
k

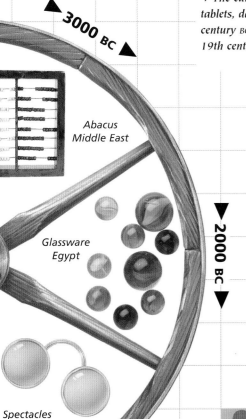

▲ **3000 BC** ▲

*Abacus
Middle East*

*Glassware
Egypt*

▼ **2000 BC** ▼

*Spectacles
Italy*

▲ **AD 1290** ▲

▲ *The wheel was first invented over 5000 years ago. Early wheels were made from wooden planks. Around 2000 BC spoked wheels, used for chariots and carts, were invented.*

Lifting water

Archimedes (c.287–212 BC), an ancient Greek mathematician and inventor from Sicily (then ruled by Greece), invented the water-screw. This is a mechanical device used for raising water from a lower to a higher level. Known as the Archimedean screw, it is still used to irrigate fields in the Middle East. The same principle is used in the grain loader of a combine harvester.

▶ *A large screw is set at an angle in a tube that is open at both ends. When the screw is turned, water fills the air pockets between the twists and gradually travels upwards until it pours out of the top.*

l
m
n
o
p
q

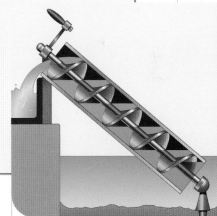

▶▶ **Read further › combine harvesters**
pg14 (r10)

r

INVENTIVE

- By about 1450 BC, the Egyptians were making glass bottles, shaping the glass by blowing it into moulds. Glassblowing (using air to shape very hot glass) was probably invented in Syria about 10 BC.

- To build the city of Jericho in Jordan about 8000 years ago, bricks were made from clay baked in the sun. About 5500 years ago, bricks were fired in a kiln to make them harder and waterproof.

s
t
u

Check it out!

- http://www.enchantedlearning.com/inventors

v

w

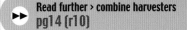

The first scissors were used in Europe and Asia about 3000 years ago

Everyday inventions

MANY INVENTIONS, such as toothbrushes, pens, paperclips, clocks, saucepans, sandwiches and umbrellas, have become so much a part of our everyday lives that we take them for granted. These inventions may not have changed the world in the same way as the wheel *(see pg9 [n16])* or light bulb, but many, such as CDs, enable us to benefit from inventions that harness new technology.

IT'S A FACT

• Toilet paper was invented in the United States by Joseph Cayetty in 1857. British inventor Walter Alcock first manufactured a toilet roll in 1879.

• The ancient Romans first invented a form of central heating about 2000 years ago.

Wish you were here

Postcards were invented in 1861 by John P. Charlton. They were first printed in 1869 by Emmanual Hermann of Vienna, who thought they would be cheaper to send by post than a normal letter in an envelope. The first picture postcard was produced in 1894.

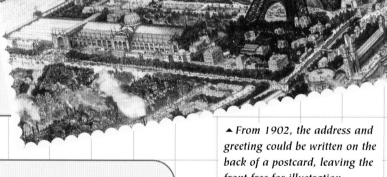

▲ *From 1902, the address and greeting could be written on the back of a postcard, leaving the front free for illustration. Previously the text had to go on the front, with the picture.*

Grandfather clock

The pendulum clock was first thought of by Galileo Galilei of Italy (1564–1642), but his idea was not developed until the 1600s by Christian Huygens (1629–1695) of Holland. He used the pendulum – a heavy weight that swings back and forth pulled by a magnetic force – to regulate the ticking. The pendulum swings continuously, keeping the clock in time.

◀ *Grandfather clocks were named after the song 'My Grandfather's Clock', written by Henry Clay Work in 1876.*

▶▶ **Read further › watch pg8 (r19)**

 Check it out!

• http://www.worldalmanac forkids.com/explore/inventions. html

• http://www.ideafinder.com/ history/inventions/story055.htm

Umbrellas

The word umbrella comes from the Italian word *ombrella*, meaning 'little shade'. It is a very old invention, used first by the Egyptians about 4000 years ago as a sunshade. Early Chinese umbrellas, used from about AD 400, were made from heavily oiled paper. The Greeks introduced the umbrella into Europe, where it became popular in the 16th century to protect from rain as well as sun. Umbrella coverings gradually changed from sticky, oiled paper, silk or linen to cotton, alpaca and waterproof nylon.

▲ *The modern folding umbrella with metal spokes was invented by Englishman Samuel Fox in 1874.*

**▶▶ Read further › fabrics
pg18 (d2)**

INVENTIVE

• Post-it® notes were invented in the 1970s by Art Fry. He used Spencer Silver's glue, which did not stick permanently.

• Felt pens were invented in Japan in 1962. Ink flows through a fibre pad when it touches a writing surface.

Rolling writing

The biro was named after Hungarian journalist László Biro in 1938. He found a way of creating ball-point pens, which work by using tiny balls inside the pens, instead of nibs, to roll ink over the paper. László and his brother Georg invented a smudge-proof ink that did not clog up the point of the pen. After fleeing to Argentina during World War II, László's pens were sold first in Buenos Aires, and then worldwide, from 1945.

▶ *In the 1950s, Frenchman Marcel Bich created a cheap, disposable version of the pen. He founded the Bic® empire.*

**▶▶ Read further › pens
pg11 (j22)**

▶ *The track on a CD is 5 km long and thinner than a human hair.*

Fast food

In the mid 1700s, Englishman John Montague, the fourth Earl of Sandwich, was so keen on playing card games that he did not want to stop for meals. Servants brought him meals of meat placed between pieces of buttered bread, so they were easy to eat. The Earl could then eat his meals as he continued to play.

Storing sound

First made by James Russell in 1965, and later developed by the research team of the Philips company in the 1970s, the compact disc (CD) has better sound quality than tapes or records and can hold up to 75 minutes of sound. CDs work by storing sound as a coded signal, made up of 0s and 1s, that can be 'read' by a laser beam. The pits or grooves on the CD break the light from the laser beam into flashes of light that are converted into electrical signals. When fed into loudspeakers, the signals turn back into sound again.

**▶▶ Read further › DVDs
pg34 (t16)**

a
b
c
d
e
f
g
h
i
j
k
l
m
n
o
p
q
r
s
t
u
v
w

In the home

TODAY THERE are many devices to help with cooking and cleaning in the home. Inventions such as the iron have been used for centuries, but some labour-saving devices were only possible after the invention of small electric motors by American Joseph Henry – first fitted to domestic appliances in 1899 – which convert electric energy into motion. Once electricity was available in homes from around 1900, electrical items such as sewing machines *(see pg19 [c29])* and hairdryers became widely used. Today, electric motors are in appliances such as refrigerators and lawnmowers. Microwave ovens and smoke alarms contain computer chips or sensors that respond and react to commands quickly and efficiently.

IT'S A FACT

• The first pop-up toaster was invented in the United States about 70 years ago.

• The first electric kettle was designed by the Russell-Hobbs company in 1955. A thermostat switched off the kettle by breaking the electric circuit when the water reached boiling point.

Keeping cool

Until the 19th century, blocks of ice were used to cool food and in the 1830s, ice-making machines compressed air, which then expanded through a valve. In 1858 Frenchman Ferdinand Carré invented liquid refrigerant, a type of which is still used today. The refrigerant flows continually around the pipes at the back of the fridge, taking heat from the interior and transferring it to the outside, where it escapes through a grill into the air.

Early irons

In the 8th century, the Chinese used pans full of hot charcoal to smooth silk – these were the first irons. The most common iron, used from the 18th century, was the sad iron – 'sad' meant heavy. The irons had to be heated over a fire. The first electric iron, invented in 1882 by Henry Seeley in New York, used a wire element heated by electricity. This iron could not be used in many homes at the time however, because most did not have electricity. The first electric steam iron was introduced in 1926 by New York company, Eldec.

Read further > fabric pg18 [d2]

◄ 'Sad' irons had to be used in pairs so that one iron was heating over a fire while the other was in use.

▲ Early 20th century electric refrigerators were made in the USA from about 1915.

Read further > heating food pg13 [b30]

Josephine Cochrane invented the first efficient dishwasher in 1886

Grass cutting

The first lawnmower, created in 1831 by Edwin Budding, was pulled by horses wearing rubber boots to stop them damaging the lawn. In 1896, W.J. Stephenson-Peach designed the first petrol-driven mower, which was made by the Ransomes company in 1902. With the arrival of electric lawnmowers, different varieties were made – some of them, such as the Flymo®, even hovered above the grass.

▶ *On the first lawnmower, sharp blades to cut the grass rotated around a horizontal bar.*

▶▶ Read further › electricity
pg21 (j32)

Speedy heating

Microwave

Deflector

Microwave ovens were developed in 1953 by Percy Spencer. He was working on ways of using invisible microwaves to detect enemy planes during World War II. Spencer noticed that the waves had melted a chocolate bar that was in his pocket and realized they could be useful in cooking. Microwaves heat up food by making tiny particles of water in the food vibrate so fast that they give off heat. The microwaves do not contain any heat themselves.

▶▶ Read further › waves
pg24 (q11)

◀ *Microwave ovens have a rotating tray that turns the food, while the deflector directs the microwaves onto it.*

INVENTIVE

• Francis Gabe's 1940's invention, a self-cleaning house was not a great success! Waterproof furniture is sprayed with water and soap and then huge air-blowers dry off everything. The whole clean-up takes about an hour.

• In 1589, Sir John Harington designed a flushing toilet but few houses had a water supply or drains. Two hundred years later, Joseph Bramah made the first widely-used toilet based on a design by Alexander Cummings.

Saving lives

The first smoke alarm was designed in 1967 by the American company BRK Electronics. Smoke alarms work by using light or low-level radioactivity to detect the tiny smoke particles produced as a fire starts. When this happens the alarm makes a loud piercing noise to warn people.

From fire to fans

Before 1920 people dried their hair using the heat from the sun or an open fire. The first hairdryers made in America were called the Race and the Cyclone. In 1925, the Sol electric dryer had a simple heater and small fan. It was made of lightweight aluminium with a wooden handle, and had two levels of heat. Modern hairdryers are more compact than the earlier models and give out much higher levels of heat.

▶ *A hairdryer contains a long, thin coil of wire that produces heat. The heat is powered by electricity and is channelled through the barrel at the end.*

Check it out!

• http://www.sjsu.edu/depts/Museum/henry.html
• http://www.worldalmanacforkids.com/explore/inventions
• http://www.home.howstuffworks.com/hair-dryer.htm

The first vacuum cleaners were so big they had to be towed from house to house by horses!

a b c d e f g h i j k l m n o p q r s t u v w

Food and farming

P EOPLE HAVE been inventing ways of growing, cooking and preserving food for centuries. But after the invention of ploughs (see pg8 [t9]), there was little advance in farm machinery until the 18th century in Britain – a period known as the Industrial Revolution – when new machinery began to develop rapidly, leading to such inventions as the combine harvester. Food and drink, such as sugar and tea, have been available for centuries, but burgers, crisps and bubble gum are more recent inventions, dating from the 19th century.

● IT'S A FACT

• Coca-Cola was first created by Dr John S. Pemberton in 1886. He mixed syrup with soda water, to make it bubbly, in a brass kettle.

• The latest combine harvesters have soundproofed cabs and even air-conditioning.

Seed stored in hopper

◄ *Jethro Tull's seed drill made harvesting easier as seeds were sown in rows.*

Seeds fall down tubes into holes in soil

Drill digs holes

● Sowing seeds

Three thousand years ago, people living in Babylonia (present day Iraq) used a simple device for sowing seeds, which dropped them down a tube on top of a plough. In 1660, Taddeo Calvani invented the first seed drill, which consisted of a container with holes in the bottom mounted on a cart. The vibrations of the cartwheels shook the seeds out through the holes. In 1701, English farmer Jethro Tull invented a much more efficient version. The seeds dropped down tubes into furrows in the soil and were sown in regular rows. This made it much more likely that seeds would take root, because they had plenty of room in the soil to grow.

▶▶ Read further > ploughs
pg8 [j8]

● Harvesting

A combine harvester combines the two stages of harvesting: cutting the crop and separating the grain. The first combine harvester was designed in 1836 by Americans Hiram Moore and John Hascall. It was pulled by horses.

▼ *The first motorized combine harvesters, produced in 1961, increased the speed at which crops are harvested.*

▶▶ Read further > harvesting
pg9 [k28]

Cans to store food were invented about 45 years before can openers were invented!

1   2   3   4   5   6   7   8   9   10   11   12   13   14   15   16   17   18   19

▶▶ **Read further › wheels**
pg9 (u22)

● Shopping on wheels

Sylvan Goldman of Oklahoma, USA invented the shopping trolley in 1936 to persuade people to buy more in his grocery store. He had noticed that people stopped shopping when their hand-held baskets were full. His first design, based on a folding chair with wheels on the legs, one basket on the seat and another just above the wheels, was a simple idea, but very effective. Goldman's invention came at the right time because supermarkets were starting to be built in America. His invention made him a millionaire.

● From pots to burgers

In 1904 Fletcher Davis invented the hamburger. He was a potter by trade and became involved in the burger business by cooking at pottery shows. He also ran a small café in east Texas. His burgers were the classic burger made from ground beef, served on toasted bread and garnished with salad, mustard and mayonnaise.

▸ *The word 'cheeseburger' was patented in 1944 by Louis Ballast, after he grilled a slice of cheese on top of a burger at his Colorado drive-in.*

● INVENTIVE

• The popsicle was invented by 11-year-old American Frank Epperson in 1905 after he left a fruit drink out overnight (with a stirrer in it) and the drink froze. The popsicle was originally called the Epsicle, after its inventor.

• Inventors are trying to grow square tomatoes, which would be much easier to stack in boxes for shipping.

● Double bubble

Bubble gum is extra-strong gum that can be blown into bubbles. First invented in 1906 by American Frank Henry Fleer, it was called Blibber-Blubber. It was too sticky – when it popped it was very difficult to peel off the face – and therefore unsuccessful. In 1928, Walter E. Deimer invented a better mixture for bubble gum, which he called 'Dubble Bubble'.

◂ *Bubble gum is made in all sorts of shapes, colours and sizes, from simple, round spheres to novelty shapes, such as cigars.*

◂ *Farmers across the world seek ways to increase their produce: GM is one way they can do this.*

● Genetically modified

One of the most controversial scientific discoveries of the 20th century is the genetic modification (GM) of foods. The genes of every living organism can be altered to change its characteristics. For example, farmers can add anti-pest genes to crops, which enables them to survive longer or grow unusually large.

🌐 **Check it out!**

• http://www.ideafinder.com/history/inventions/story026.htm

▶▶ **Read further › genes**
pg34 (b15)

Ice-cream sodas were created in 1874 when someone accidentally dropped ice-cream into a glass of soda

22 23 24 25 26 27 28 29 30 31 32 33 34 35 36 37 38 39

Fun and games

SOME INVENTIONS make the world more fun to live in. Entertainment and games, such as fireworks and playing cards, were invented centuries ago. The ancient Egyptian king Tutankhamun had toys buried with him inside his tomb. The ancient Greeks and Romans played with dolls and spinning tops. Other inventions, such as the rocking horse, date from the 1700s. More recently, science has influenced the invention of toys with the use of pendulums and springs in toys such as the jack-in-the-box. Electricity, batteries and computers have since revolutionized toy-making, which has lead to the creation of robots and computer games.

IT'S A FACT

• Yo-yos made of stone and thought to be more than 3000 years old were found in Greece.

• In the 1970s, toy manufacturers first used radio waves to control model aeroplanes and boats.

• Meccano (metal construction set containing nuts, bolts, gears and blocks) was invented in 1901 by Frank Hornby whilst watching a construction crane working.

Rocking horses

The rocking horse was invented in 1780 as a toy that children could ride on without risking their safety. However, only wealthy families could afford to buy them until the Industrial Revolution in Britain. This saw the new, wealthy, middle class. Early Victorian rocking horses were sat upon deeply curved bow rockers but these were later considered unsafe. In about 1880, Philip Marqua of Cincinnati, USA, invented a safety stand to replace the dangerous bow rockers.

Read further › industrial revolution
pg14 (d2)

Check it out!
• http://www.factmonster.com/ipka/A0768872.html
• http://www.inventionatplay.org/inventors_main.html

▲ *Early rocking horses were English dapple-grey in colour and rocked on wooden bow rockers.*

▶ *This LEGO pirate ship uses about 100,000 bricks. LEGO towers up to 20 m high have been built using about 300,000 bricks.*

Read further › bricks
pg9 (r27)

Building bricks

LEGO bricks were invented by Ole Kirk Christiansen of Denmark in 1934. Christiansen devised the name LEGO from the Danish words *Leg godt*, which means 'to play well'. He developed the toy and added studs to the LEGO bricks in 1955 so that they would fit into one another. This made it easy to build the bricks into tall, rigid structures with the weight pushing down through all the bricks.

Enough rope has been included in Cluedo sets to encircle the whole world

◀ After gunpowder had been used for fireworks for 300 years, the Chinese began to use it in warfare. They invented rockets fuelled by gunpowder in the 13th century, which helped them to defeat an invading Mongol army.

Lights in the sky

Fireworks were invented by the Chinese about 1000 years ago, after the invention of gunpowder. Original Chinese fireworks were only one colour, yellow. However, new ingredients, such as magnesium and aluminium added in the 19th century, made a greater range of colours possible. The most popular form of firework, the rocket, works by being pushed high up into the sky by the jet of fire thrown out behind it when it burns rapidly.

◀ When fireworks explode, their chemical energy changes into light, sound, heat and movement energy.

▶▶ **Read further > explosives** pg21 (s33); pg32 (m8)

Playing to win

Playing cards are thought to have been invented in about AD 1000 in China. By the 1200s, card games were played in Italy and the game of skill and chance spread across Europe. When they were invented, cards were long and narrow with symbols and figures.

Teddy bears

The first teddy bears, made in the United States in 1903, were based on a bear from a cartoon about President Roosevelt, whose nickname was Teddy. He had spared the life of a real bear cub whilst out on a hunting trip. Toy bears were later made with squeaks or growls that worked when air flowed over plastic strips to make sounds when shaken.

▶▶ **Read further > cartoons** pg25 (q27)

▲ The teddy bear became the most successful soft toy ever invented.

◀ The four suits on playing cards – hearts, clubs, diamonds and spades – originated in France in the 1500s when the practice of card playing spread across Europe.

INVENTIVE

• In the 18th century, mechanical toys with moving parts, such as walking dolls, became the new craze.

• Slinkys, springs that 'walk' down stairs, were invented in 1943.

Roller skates were first seen when the inventor skated into a ballroom playing the violin before crashing into a mirror!

a b c d e f g h i j k l m n o p q r s t u v w

Textile industry

SOME CLOTHES and fabrics have been around for centuries. Embroidery dates back to the ancient Egyptians, who were also wearing shoes about 6000 years ago, though shoes were not mass-produced until the 1890s. The invention of the spinning jenny and sewing machine and the use of synthetic materials such as nylon in the 1930s has dramatically increased consumers' choice in fabric and textiles. After World War II, German manufacturer Adolf Dassler, founder of Adidas, developed trainers using leftover tent canvas and rubber from fuel tanks. More recent inventions, such as zips, velcro, bikinis and T-shirts, date from the 1900s.

IT'S A FACT

• The first raincoat was invented by Charles Mackintosh in 1823, after he made a waterproof cloth.

• Nylon was first manufactured by American W. H. Carothers in 1935. About 64 million pairs of nylon stockings were sold in the first year of manufacture, 1939.

▼ The spinning jenny enabled yarn (thread) to be spun onto eight spindles at once. Thus the production of material became much faster.

Embroidery

The earliest known fabric samples date from about 5000 years ago. They showed that people sewed coloured stitches by hand over woven threads. The ancient Egyptians, Babylonians, Phoenicians and Hebrews used embroidery to decorate their clothes. One of the most famous pieces of embroidery is the Bayeux Tapestry, a wall-hanging nearly 70 m long, embroidered to describe how William of Normandy became King of England in 1066. Labourious hand embroidery was aided in the 1800s when embroidery machines, based on the newly invented sewing machine (see pg 19 [c30]), were invented. The invention of computers has enabled the embroidery process to speed up dramatically.

◀ The Bayeux Tapestry was embroidered by hand after 1066, using eight shades of wool on a bare linen background. It took about 11 years to complete.

Read further > hieroglyphics / sewing / computers
pg9 [b22]; pg19 [b22]; pg25 [h22]

Spinning jenny

The first spinning wheel originated in India about 1000 years ago. In the 19th century industrial revolution, machines such as the spinning jenny, built by Englishman James Hargreaves in 1767, enabled thread to be spun by twisting fibres together quickly. This had previously been done using a hand-held spindle (a weighted stick) that twisted fibres as it spun round but it was slow. The spinning jenny had several spindles that could be moved by one driving wheel.

Read further > wheel
pg9 [u22]

Check it out!

• http://www.centuryinshoes.com/home.html
• http://www.fashion-era.com/fitness_fashion_after_1960.htm

Sewing machines

The first sewing machine was invented in 1830 by a French tailor, Barthélemy Thimonnier. He made chain stitches (interlocking loops) from one thread. Elias Howe developed a machine in 1846 that used bobbins containing the thread and a rotating handle to manoeuvre the fabric but it was unsuccessful. In 1850, American Isaac Singer patented a machine that used the features from each of the previous machines, which became very successful. Domestic sewing machines have increased in speed from 20 stitches per minute to around 1000 stitches per minute.

▶▶ **Read further > spinning**
pg18 (n13)

Bikini

The invention of the bikini in 1946 by American fashion designers followed the American government's order to cut the fabric used in women's swimwear by at least one-tenth to reduce waste during World War II.

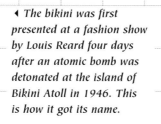

◀ *The bikini was first presented at a fashion show by Louis Reard four days after an atomic bomb was detonated at the island of Bikini Atoll in 1946. This is how it got its name.*

INVENTIVE

• Jeans were invented in around 1850 by Oscar Levi Strauss. He invented them for miners in the California gold rush as they needed hardwearing clothes.

• Copper studs on the pockets of jeans were invented to prevent splits, which were caused by keeping heavy tools in the pockets.

Zip it up

In 1893, American inventor Whitcomb L. Judson invented the zip (or zipper). He first thought of it as a way of fastening shoes rather than clothes. His zips were not very reliable: they kept jamming or flying open without warning. Eventually, in 1913, a Canadian engineer called Gideon Sundback produced zips similar to those we use today. His zip was called the Talon Slide Fastener and was first used on a boot called the zipper (from where the name came).

▼ *The zip had two rows of teeth opened or shut by a slider, which were all attached to flexible, parallel tapes.*

Velcro

Velcro was invented in 1957 when Georges de Mestral studied the burdock seed heads that had stuck to his clothes and saw under a microscope that they were covered in tiny hooks. Loom-maker Jakob Muller helped de Mestral to realize his invention. Velcro is French for 'hooked velvet' and is made of two nylon strips: one covered in thousands of tiny loops and the other with tiny hooks.

▶ *Ice-skating boots use strips of velcro pressed together to hold the boot securely in place. The hooks and loops make a tight seal that can easily be ripped apart again.*

Pockets were not invented until the 17th century: they started out as a small opening in the seam of a pair of trousers

22 23 24 25 26 27 28 29 30 31 32 33 34 35 36 37 38 39

a
b
c
d
e
f
g
h
i
j
k
l
m
n
o
p
q
r
s
t
u
w

Power it up

INVENTIONS THAT use sources of natural power have been developed over thousands of years to make our lives easier. The ancient Greeks and Romans used water mills to grind grain and olives more than 2000 years ago. The invention of the steam engine and ways to control gas and create electricity revolutionized mechanical movement and power. Today, coal and oil is burnt in power stations to make electricity and to power engines for transport, but these sources of energy will eventually run out. We need therefore to utilise natural energy – solar, wind and water power are everlasting sources.

IT'S A FACT

• About one-fifth of the world's electricity is generated by hydro-electric power.

• It is estimated that we have enough coal to last about 1500 years and enough oil and natural gas to last for about 60 years.

▸ Before automatic timers were installed in the early 1900s, gas lamps were lit using long torches.

Gas lighting

In 1792, Englishman William Murdock invented a lighting system based on heating coal in a closed vessel and piping the gas it made to make light. He later developed a system for producing and storing gas. In the 19th century, coal gas provided many towns with energy for lighting and heating. In 1885, Austrian Carl Auer invented the gas mantle: this was a mesh of carbonized cotton that glowed brightly when heated and was used in street lamps.

First engines

The first practical steam engine, invented by Englishman Thomas Savery in 1698, pumped out water from flooded coal mines. Savery's engine cooled and condensed steam (a gas) into water, leaving a vacuum (no gas), which sucked up the flood water (a liquid). In 1712, Englishman Thomas Newcomen built an improved steam engine. The steam and the vacuum moved a piston up and down, which rocked a crossbeam, which in turn worked a water pump. In 1765, James Watt made improvements to Newcomen's engine. He added a chamber to cool and condense the steam to change it back into water so that the engine did not have to be heated and cooled all the time.

►► Read further > pumping water pg9 (k28)

◂ James Watt made the piston on the steam engine move like a wheel, using gears and a connecting rod.

Check it out!

• http://www.bbc.co.uk/history/ historic_figures/newcomen_ thomas.shtml

Water power

The oldest known dam, made of soil and stones, was built across the Garawi valley in Egypt about 5000 years ago. Modern arch dams were invented in the 1850s by French scientist François Zola. They resist the pushing force of the water because their shape pushes the water down. In a gravity dam, the great weight of the material they are built from stops the water from pushing its way through.

▲ *Water falling from inside a gravity dam can push turbine wheels around to generate electricity. This is called hydro-electric power (hydro means water).*

Read further › wind power
pg31 [o28]

▼ *In 1882, Thomas Edison's factories made 100,000 light bulbs. By 1900 over 45 million were needed in the US alone to light towns and cities.*

Read further › solar-powered cars
pg31 [n22]

Power of the Sun

The Sun beams a vast amount of energy to the Earth. This energy can be collected and concentrated by photovoltaic (solar) cells to generate electricity. The manufacture of photovoltaic cells was only possible from the mid-1900s when American scientists G.L. Pearson, D.M. Chapin and C.S. Fuller developed a solar battery made of tiny solar cells. Solar power is safe and environmentally friendly because it does not cause pollution of any kind.

▶ *Solar cells can turn about 15 per cent of the sunlight that falls on them into electrical energy. Scientists hope to improve this percentage.*

▼ *Oil refineries produce enough oil to fuel about half the energy we use.*

Electric city

Before gas and electricity were used, people relied on oil and gas lamps and candles to provide artificial light. The electric light bulb, invented by American scientists Thomas Edison and Joseph Swan in about 1879, was air-tight so that it could burn for longer. Inside a light bulb, a tiny, thin coiled wire called a filament gets so hot that it glows brightly, giving off light when electricity tries to squeeze through it. The flow of electricity causes the wire filament to glow brightly inside the airless bulb. Made of a type of metal called tungsten, the filament can get very hot without melting.

Read further › gas lamps
pg20 [i14]

Drilling for oil

The Chinese first drilled for oil 2000 years ago using bamboo and bronze pipes. In 1844, Englishman Robert Beart introduced rotary drilling using steam engines. A drilling bit on the end of a hollow steel pipe forced up the rock (and oil) by pumping water down the pipe. The first offshore oil well was built off the American coast.

INVENTIVE

• In 1867 Alfred Nobel invented dynamite (named after the Greek word for power, *dynamis*). In his will, he requested that it should not be used in war.

• Five prizes (Nobel Prizes) are awarded each year for: physics, chemistry, medicine, literature and the promotion of peace.

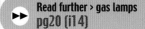

Modern light bulbs have a tungsten filament that heats up to about 3000°C

a b c d e f g h i j k l m n o p q r s t u v w

On the move

IT'S A FACT

• The world's first motorway was built in 1921 near Berlin, Germany. It was only 9.8 km long.

• The Model T Ford was the first car to be mass-produced. More than 15 million were made between 1908 and 1927.

• Within the next decade, the Airbus 360 (the 'super jumbo') could be flying. It will weigh nearly 600 tonnes and carry more than 600 passengers.

AROUND 150 YEARS ago, there were no high-speed trains, jumbo jets, or fast cars. The first bicycles, built in the early 1800s with wheels of wood, iron, and later solid rubber, were too uncomfortable to be successful. But cycling became popular after the invention of the pneumatic tyre in 1888. The internal combustion engine, invented in 1860, led to the invention of cars, planes, ships and trains in the 1900s. Today, supersonic aircraft, racing cars, helicopters, hovercraft, 'bullet' trains and even spacecraft allow people to travel across the world at high speeds.

▼ Petrol engines, such as those used in most cars today, were invented by German Gottlieb Daimler and Karl Benz in 1883.

Engines

The invention of the internal combustion engine in 1859 by Belgian inventor Étienne Lenoir, revolutionized transport. Lenoir's two-stroke engine used ignited fuel – usually a mixture of coal, gas and air – by a spark of electricity, which burned (combustion). The explosion moved the pistons in the cylinder and waste gases were pushed out at the second stroke. Today, most cars use the much faster four-stroke petrol engine, which was developed in 1876 by German inventor, Nikolaus Otto. The four-stroke engine consists of intake, compression, power and exhaust.

▶▶ Read further > pistons pg20 (L2)

Pudding tyres

Scottish vet John Dunlop invented air-filled (pneumatic) tyres in 1888. He experimented with a water-filled hosepipe wrapped around his son's bicycle tyres. The air-filled tyres were first known as 'pudding tyres'. They gave a faster and smoother ride than vehicles that used solid rubber tyres.

◄ Early bicycles, such as the penny farthing, had solid rubber tyres and were uncomfortable to ride.

Getting off the ground

In 1903, the two American Wright brothers, Orville and Wilbur, made the first-ever powered flight at Kitty Hawk, North Carolina, lasting 12 seconds and covering 36 m. Planes are able to fly because the tops of the wings are curved and so the air that is pushed over the top of the wings is forced to speed up and stretch out, reducing its pressure and pulling from above. The pull from above is called 'lift'. The world's biggest airliner today is the Boeing 747 or 'jumbo jet'.

▶▶ Read further > Airbus 360 / engine
pg22 (f15; o2)

▶ *The jumbo jet weighs more than 300 tonnes and can carry about 500 passengers. It flies at up to 1600 km/h on flights lasting up to 14 hours non-stop.*

FIRST ON THE ROAD

Invention	Country	Year on the road
• Steam tractor	France	1769
• Steam coach	UK	1801
• Steam dredger	USA	1805
• Gas carriage	UK	1820s
• Petrol car	Germany	1885

Cushions of air

English engineer Christopher Cockerell invented the hovercraft in 1955, but the first large hovercraft was not launched until 1969. Hovercraft float above the waves on a cushion of air. Large fans blow air underneath the craft and a 'skirt' at the bottom stops air leaking out.

▶ *As the hovercraft travels above the water, there is no friction to slow it down, so it can travel at up to 120 km/h.*

▶▶ Read further > pneumatic tyres
pg22 (q13)

Floating trains

Magnetic levitation (Maglev) trains were first thought of by American engineer Robert Goddard in 1909. However, the design was patented in 1934 by German engineer Hermann Kemper. Maglev trains do not have wheels: instead they float above the track using magnetism.

▶▶ Read further > Solo Trek
pg34 (r8)

🌐 **Check it out!**

- http://www.worldalmanacfor kids.com/explore/inventions. html
- http://www.pbs.org/wgbh/ amex/kids/tech1900
- http://invention.psychology. msstate.edu/air_main.shtml

▶ *The Maglev train and the track both contain powerful magnets, which repel each other, lifting the train up so that it hovers above the rail. The magnets work when electricity flows through them.*

A Japanese engineer invented a suitcase that converts into a small go-kart-like car that travels at 19 km/h!

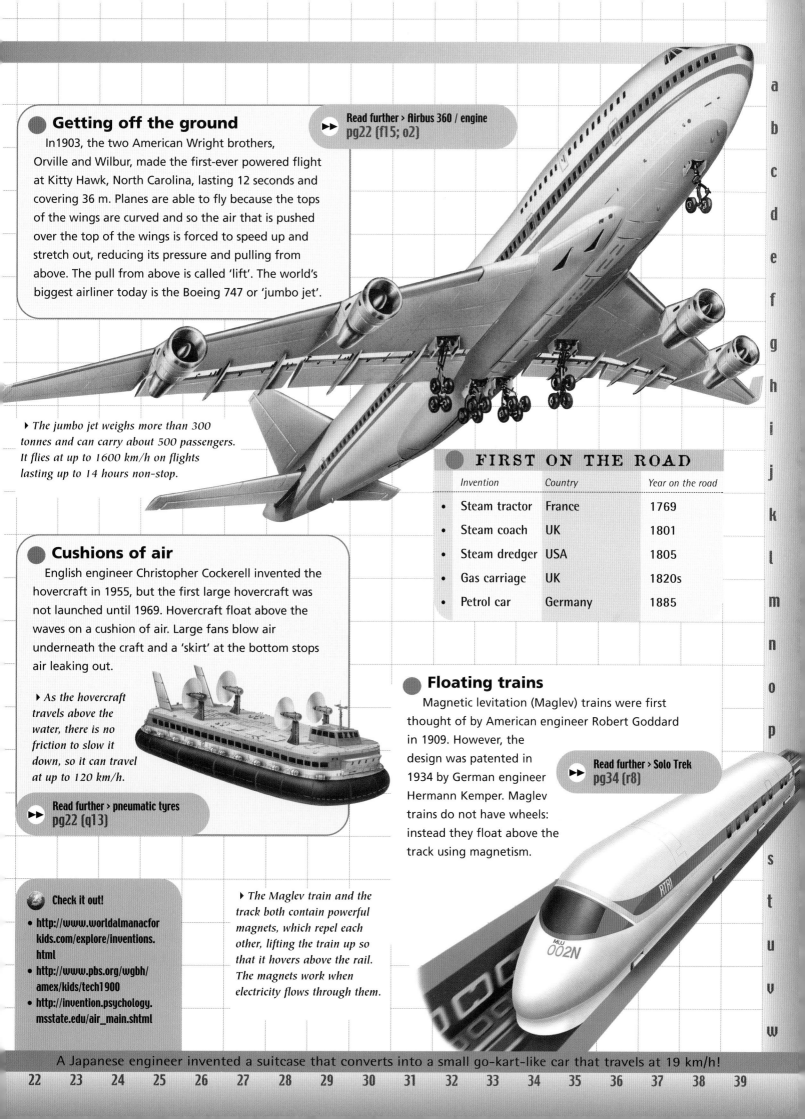

Mass media

ELECTRONIC DEVICES such as radios, televisions and computers change electrical signals into sounds and pictures. Inside these devices are electronic components that control the way electricity flows around a circuit, making it perform particular tasks. Early radios and televisions used valves to switch tiny electrical signals, but these were large and used up lots of electricity. In the 1940s American scientists invented transistors that worked like valves but were smaller and more efficient. By the 1960s, transistors and other electronic components were all placed in one chip of silicon 5 mm square. Today microchips control computers and many other devices.

● IT'S A FACT

• In 1887 Thomas Edison invented the phonograph, the first machine to record sound and play it back.

• Game Boys were developed in 1989 by Nintendo to allow video games to be carried around.

● Televisions

The first televisions relied on the cathode ray tube, invented in 1897 by German physicist Karl Braun. These fire streams of electrons – tiny particles that are parts of atoms – at a specially coated screen to make it glow. The first television was presented in 1926 by John Logie Baird. In a colour television there are three electron streams: red, blue and green. These light up phosphor dots on the screen, which blend to form a full colour image.

▲ *Some flat screen TVs invented in Japan in the 1980s, use liquid crystal displays instead of cathode ray tubes.*

● Early computers

In 1823, English mathematician Charles Babbage invented the first type of computer – the 'difference engine'. It proved too complex to complete and in 1834 Babbage began constructing his 'analytical engine' in which data was fed into the engine by punched cards. The results were designed to be printed out. Though it was never built in full, as it would have been the size of a small train, Babbage's idea helped others to invent the first computers.

◀ *The engine had a memory that was able to retain up to 100 40-digit numbers and a central processor to make calculations.*

Early computer
90 cm across

To scale
1 square across = 16 cm

Personal Digital Assistant
8 cm in length

● Radio revolution

In 1895, Italian inventor Marchese Guglielmo Marconi was the first person to send signals without wires. Marconi produced invisible radio waves from an electric current that changes direction thousands of times a second. In 1901 he sent radio messages across the Atlantic, from England to the USA. In 1906 people first heard voices over the radio. Today radio waves are also used in mobile phones.

▲ *Early radios were called wirelesses as they used only waves, not wires or cables, to carry sound.*

Video games

The first successful video game was invented in 1972 by American computer programer Nolan Bushnell. It was a form of electronic table tennis called *Pong*. A video game is controlled by the memory on a silicon chip computer circuit. Most systems are based on the central processing units (CPUs) used in many computers. Video games are controlled using a user control interface, such as a key pad. All game consoles use a video signal that is compatible with television.

▶▶ **Read further › games**
pg16 (d2)

▸ *In this game called* Ape Man, *a graphics processor provides texture, colour and other functions and a chip handles the sound.*

Clever computers

The first home computer was produced in 1975 by Altair in the USA, and the Apple Macintosh followed in 1984. When computers were first developed in the 1940s they filled entire rooms. The ENIAC (Electronic Numerical Integrator and Calculator), built in 1946, weighed 30 tonnes. Using 805 km of wire, it carried out 100,000 tasks per second. Computers are smaller since the invention of the transistor (electronic switch that detects electric current) in 1948 and integrated circuits in 1957. The latest iMacs are flat-screened.

▶▶ **Read further › early computers**
pg24 (m2)

▲ *A liquid crystal display (LCD) produces images on a flat screen by using electric current to control the path of light through liquid crystals and coloured filters.*

INVENTIVE

• In 1926 the first moving television picture was made by John Logie Baird, using a spinning disc with holes, invented in 1884 by Paul Nipkow.

• Baird's system was later replaced by an electronic system invented by Vladimir Zworykin in the 1920s.

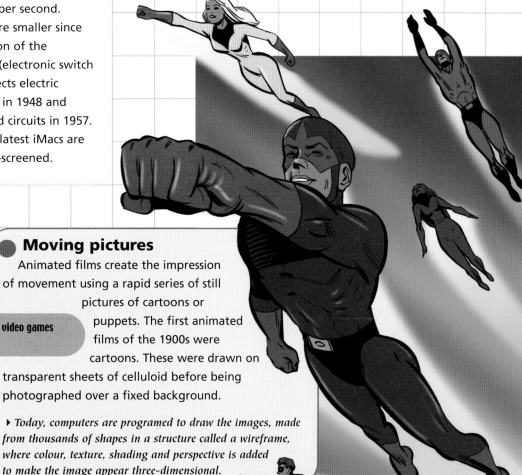

Moving pictures

Animated films create the impression of movement using a rapid series of still pictures of cartoons or puppets. The first animated films of the 1900s were cartoons. These were drawn on transparent sheets of celluloid before being photographed over a fixed background.

▶▶ **Read further › video games**
pg25 (b22)

▸ *Today, computers are programed to draw the images, made from thousands of shapes in a structure called a wireframe, where colour, texture, shading and perspective is added to make the image appear three-dimensional.*

🌐 **Check it out!**
• http://www.computerhistory.org
• http://www.greatachievements.org

Keeping in touch

IT'S A FACT

• In 1455, the first book printed by Gutenberg was the Bible.

• Sign language for the deaf was invented in 1620 by J.P. Bonnet, a tutor at the Spanish court.

UNTIL PEOPLE learned to write they were only able to communicate when speaking face to face. Information was passed verbally through the generations, often through story-telling. About 5000 years ago the Sumerians and ancient Egyptians invented writing. Then about 4000 years later, the Chinese invented printing by hand. The mechanical printing press was invented about 500 years ago in Europe by Johannes Gutenberg. Other communication methods, such as Braille and Morse code, were invented in the 1800s. Today e-mails, telephones and fax machines connect people all over the world, and because of the Internet, information is easier to access than ever before.

▼ The printing press enabled newspapers and books to be read by more people.

Printing

Before printing was invented, books were copied by hand. Invented in China before AD 868, 'letterpress' printing used letters and pictures carved from blocks of wood, clay or ivory, which were covered with ink so that when paper was pressed on them they printed the raised carving. Peking blacksmith Pi-Sheng invented movable type (individual letters on reusable blocks). In 1436 German Johannes Gutenberg invented typecasting, which made large amounts of movable type quickly and cheaply. In 1886, the linotype machine automatically cast complete lines of type from molten metal. Today, computers are used to input and print type and images.

►► Read further › ink pg11 (b33)

Clues to the past

The ancient Egyptians used written pictures and symbols, called hieroglyphics, instead of words. They used these hieroglyphics for 3500 years until about AD 400 when Greek became their written language. The Rosetta Stone, discovered in 1799, written in both hieroglyphics and Greek, provided the key to translating hieroglyphics.

►► Read further › picture writing pg9 (b22)

◄ Each hieroglyph (symbol or picture) represented an object or a sound. In total, there were about 700 different hieroglyphs.

COMMUNICATION

Invention	Year first used
• Writing	about 3500 BC
• Paper	AD 105
• Numbers 0 to 9	about 500
• Mechanical clock	1000s
• Printing press	1400s

Optical fibres carry information about 30 per cent faster than the electrical signals carried by copper telephone cables

1   2   3   4   5   6   7   8   9   10   11   12   13   14   15   16   17   18   19

Dot writing

In 1829, Frenchman Louis Braille invented a six-dot coded system of raised dots that could be used by the blind to read. Louis Braille was accidentally blinded at the age of three. When he was ten, he was shown a way of writing messages with raised dots, designed for soldiers to use at night. Braille simplified it so it was easier to read with the fingertips. Braille is still used worldwide today.

▼ *Braille is made up of different patterns of six dots, each pattern representing a letter and some short words such as 'the'.*

▶▶ **Read further › symbols**
pg9 (b22)

Dots and dashes

In 1838 Samuel Morse and Alfred Vail stopped and started an electric current along wires (or telegraphs) to communicate. Named Morse code, the short (on) bursts were the dots, and the longer (off) bursts were the dashes. In 1844, the first telegraph line opened between Baltimore and Washington, DC, enabling messages that would normally take weeks by post, to be sent instantly. Within 30 years, telegraphs covered the globe. Morse code is still used by the Navy today.

Long and short bleeps tapped into telegraph machine

Electric current

Message travels along telegraph wires to recipient

▲ *As an electric current running along a wire is stopped and started, the on and off bursts form coded messages.*

▶▶ **Read further › radio**
pg24 (q11)

Telephones old and new

Telephones were invented by Scottish-born American Alexander Graham Bell in 1876. Bell discovered how to change sound vibrations in the human voice into electrical signals, which he sent along wires to a receiver. Today, pulses of light send telephone calls down fibre optic cables, and electrical signals are sent along copper cables. The word 'telephone' comes from the Greek words for 'far' and 'sound'.

◀ *Mobile phones, invented in the 1980s, send digital radio signals to base stations, which send the signal around a network until it reaches the right phone.*

▶▶ **Read further › satellites**
pg33 (c30)

The Internet

The Internet is a worldwide network of computers. Developed in the 1970s by American computer scientist Vinton Cerf and American engineer Robert Kahn, it connects, using phone lines, local networks of computers to special computers called gateways. Cerf and Kahn defined the Internet Protocol – the software that controls the Internet. Then, in 1989, English computer scientist Tim Berners-Lee invented the World Wide Web to share information over the Internet. At the beginning of the 21st century, more than 25 million computers were linked to the Internet, and this number continues to rise.

▶ *Internet phones allow people to 'surf' (browse) the Internet from all over the world.*

▶▶ **Read further › computers**
pg25 (h22)

To scale
1 square across = 6 cm

20 cm across

Bell's first telephone

🌐 **Check it out!**

• http://www.bbc.co.uk/arts/books/
• http://www.worldalmanacfor kids.com/explore/inventions.html

The first author to type a manuscript was Mark Twain in 1874 – he used one of the first typewriters

Medicine

● IT'S A FACT

• The smallpox vaccine has wiped out the disease worldwide.

• The first dental drills appeared in the 1860s.

FROM STETHOSCOPES and vaccinations to contact lenses and forceps, many of the medical inventions of the 19th century are still used today. Before this, there was little understanding of germs or the importance of keeping wounds clean to avoid the spread of infection. Without anaesthetics to numb the pain during surgery, patients sometimes died from shock. Patients often had to be cut open to find out what was wrong with them, until instruments such as endoscopes, invented in the 1950s, were able to see inside the body. Body scanners, heart pacemakers and plastic contact lenses have since been invented.

Magnifying lenses enable surgeons to see small details

Sharp scalpel for cutting through skin, organs and blood vessels

EEG machines monitor patient's heartbeat during operation

● Fighting infection

Vaccinations protect the body against diseases, such as smallpox, tetanus and tuberculosis. Two forms of vaccination are used today: 'active' immunization is a weak but harmless form of the disease that tricks the body into producing antibodies to fight it. 'Passive' immunization uses antibodies that are already able to fight the disease. When disease affects someone who has been vaccinated, the antibodies are ready to fight.

◄ *The first vaccine was developed by Edward Jenner, about 200 years ago, to fight smallpox.*

►► Read further › treatment pg29 (j29)

►► Read further › operation pg29 (b22)

● Ancient surgical tools

About 5000 years ago, the first saws for cutting off limbs were made from wood, bone or flint, shaped into rows of sharp teeth. Flakes of flint were fixed into straight handles of wood or bone with sticky tree resin or pitch. Bronze-age patients suffered under a sharp saw to remove limbs without anaesthetic. Forceps are metal pincers that can be used to deliver babies. A hook knife was used to extract organs from a patient's body during an operation.

Iron forceps

Hook knife

Bronze Age saw

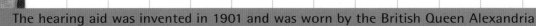
The hearing aid was invented in 1901 and was worn by the British Queen Alexandria

1 2 3 4 5 6 7 8 9 10 11 12 13 14 15 16 17 18 19

Operation

Before an operation, patients are given anaesthetics, which either cause a loss of feeling in the body, numbing the pain, or send them to sleep temporarily. In 1799, English chemist Humphrey Davey described the benefits of nitrous oxide (laughing gas). It was later used by Horace Wells in 1844.

▶▶ Read further › ancient tools
pg28 (q10)

◀ *An operating theatre is kept extremely clean to prevent the spread of infection. Surgeons wear masks, hats and coats to avoid spreading infection through breathing and from any cuts on the skin.*

Very bright lights help surgeons to see clearly during operations

Medicine

Drugs are used to treat and prevent disease and pain. The oldest list of drugs came from ancient Babylonia about 3700 years ago. Today most drugs are chemicals mixed together, or made from plants and other natural sources.

▶▶ Read further › Babylonians
pg14 (o2); pg18 (m2)

Contact lenses

Contact lenses are tiny lenses that are worn on the eye to help people see clearly. First thought of by Leonardo da Vinci around 1503, glass contact lenses were not actually made until 1887 when Adolf Eugen Fick made heavy, brown glass lenses for animals. Then in 1948, Californian optician Kevin Tuohy invented plastic lenses. In the 1970s, soft, gas-permeable lenses (that let oxygen pass through the lenses to the eyes) were made from a soft, plastic material. These float on the surface (cornea) of the eye and so can be worn for longer periods.

▶▶ Read further › spectacles
pg9 (r22)

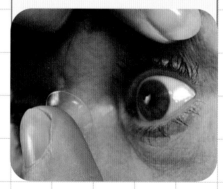

▲ *The eye has to be held wide open when putting in contact lenses.*

INVENTIVE

• The two parts of a hypodermic syringe – the needle and the plunger – were invented in 1853 by two people in two different countries: Scotland and France.

• In 1972 Godfrey Hounsfield developed a Computerised Tomography (CT) scanner, to take pictures of the inside of the body.

Pacemaker

A person's heart normally beats at about 60 to 100 times per minute but sometimes the rate becomes too fast or too slow. The rhythm can be corrected or steadied by a pacemaker, which was invented in 1958 by Swedish doctor, Ake Senning.

▸ *The battery-operated pacemaker is connected to the heart and sends it timed electrical impulses to help it beat with a regular rhythm.*

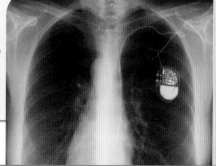

 Check it out!

• http://www.worldalmanacforkids.com/ explore/inventions.html

• http://www.enchantedlearning.com/ inventors/medicine.shtml

Before artificial false teeth were invented, people used animal teeth or bones

a b c d e f g h i j k l m n o p q r s t u v w

Earth and environment

MANY OF the inventions that have made our lives easier have not been good for the planet. The materials and power needed to make them work use up the Earth's resources and can cause pollution. Until the invention of equipment, such as satellites, it was difficult to monitor global changes. Today we know that gases and chemicals from factories and vehicles cause problems such as acid rain and global warming. Scientists are working on products that reduce damage to the environment, such as waste recycling machines, wind farms and cars that are powered by hydrogen.

IT'S A FACT

• It is possible that wind power could produce up to 20 per cent of Britain's energy.

• The Earth's temperature could rise by 4°C by the end of the 21st century, causing floods, terrible weather and food shortages.

Weather satellites

A great deal of information about the weather comes from two main kinds of satellites out in space. Polar orbiting satellites move around the Earth in a north-south direction making observations over the whole planet. Geo-stationary satellites stay above one area collecting information about that region only. Satellites are usually solar powered and beam back information about clouds and weather fronts. The first weather satellite, *Tiros 1*, built by RCA, was launched by the United States in 1960. The first geo-stationary satellite was launched over the Pacific Ocean in 1966.

Read further › satellites pg33 (c30)

◄ *Satellites provide valuable information for meteorologists (weather forecasters), cartographers (map makers) and for astronomers, as well as beaming television and telephone signals.*

INVENTIVE

• The catalytic converter, invented in 1909 by Frenchman Michel Frenkel, was developed in the 1970s when General Motors made cars that used unleaded petrol. Catalytic converters change harmful gases into harmless substances.

• Temperatures are measured in degrees Celsius or Fahrenheit. In 1701, Polish–born German physicist Daniel Fahrenheit created a scale of 180 degrees, in which the freezing point of water mixed with salt was 32°F and the boiling point (180° higher) was 212°F. In 1741, Swedish astronomer Anders Celsius reduced the scale to 100° so the freezing point of water was 0°C and the boiling point, 100°C.

Check it out!

• http://www.altenergy.org
• http://www.windpower.org/en/tour/index.htm
• http://www.epa.gov/recyclecity/

Fast roads

The first true express highways, called motorways, expressways or freeways, were the German autobahns. A network of 2110 km was planned in the 1930s and constructed by the Nazi regime by 1942 for both economic and military purposes. In the United States, the Pennsylvania turnpike and the Merritt Parkway in Connecticut were completed in 1941, followed by the building of a national system of interstate highways over many years. Motorways can be a fast and efficient way for cars and other vehicles to travel. However, traffic jams and road works can cause long delays.

▶▶ **Read further > motorways**
pg22 (b15)

▲ *Easy access to motorways increases traffic, which causes pollution.*

▼ *Newspaper recycling can save up to 75 per cent of the waste produced.*

▼ *A typical electric car averages 60 to 100 km on each charge, before running out of power.*

Reasons to recycle

The idea of recycling waste was first led by a French group called Péchiney in 1990. Every month humans throw away their own body weight in garbage: most is buried and never used again. Recycling materials prevents over-use of new materials and causes less pollution. Burning rubbish to generate electricity disposes of waste and produces energy.

Green cars

The first electric cars were developed in the United States in 1891. Electric cars do not give off harmful gases into the atmosphere so are safe for the environment. Cars that run on solar power, plant fuels or the hydrogen from water are all based on renewable sources, unlike the oil, gas and coal used to produce electricity in power stations. However, these alternative 'green' cars are still not as fast as ordinary cars and cannot store enough energy needed for long journeys.

Wind power

Windmills to capture the energy of the wind and turn it into electricity (wind turbines) were first invented in the late 1850s. They are used to pump water and generate electricity without causing harm to the environment. The Smith-Putnam machine, built in 1941 in Vermont, USA, generated huge amounts of electricity until a blade flew off.

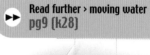
▶▶ **Read further > moving water**
pg9 (k28)

▶ *Modern metal propeller blades can extend to 100 m in length.*

▶▶ **Read further > solar power**
pg21 (j22)

a b c d e f g h i j k l m n o p q r s t u v w

Out of this world

SOME AMAZING inventions have enabled the exploration of the Solar System and beyond. At first, people could only look out into space through telescopes, invented in the 1500s. Now, telescopes in space give a much clearer view. In the 1950s scientists made rockets powerful enough to launch satellites into space. In 1969, people landed on the Moon for the first time. Space probes have now visited every planet in the Solar System except Pluto, and there have also been missions to explore asteroids and comets. In space, scientists live and work in space stations, while on the ground researchers are working towards manned exploration of planets such as Mars.

● IT'S A FACT

• The NASA space shuttle – the first re-usable spacecraft – lifts off vertically, but glides in to land horizontally, like an aircraft.

• The International Space Station orbits the Earth about 18 times a day, so astronauts watch sunrise and sunset every 45 minutes.

• Rockets orbiting the Earth need to travel at a speed of about 27,359 km/h to escape gravity, which pulls them back down towards the Earth!

● Star discoveries

Sir William Herschel invented a powerful telescope in 1789 to observe the stars and planets. He made these by making mirrors from smooth metal and eyepieces with a magnification of up to 6450 times. Along with his sister Caroline, who listed all the stars of the northern hemisphere, Herschel discovered the planet Uranus, over 2500 nebulae and more than 300 double stars (pairs of stars that appear close together in space). Herschel established the basic form of our galaxy and discovered infrared solar rays in 1801.

● Spacecraft

The first ideas on rocket propulsion date from 1903 when Russian maths teacher Konstantin Ziolkovsky suggested burning liquid fuel to propel rockets more powerfully. Spacecraft rocket engines burn fuel very quickly, producing huge amounts of hot gases that push the space shuttle up into the air. However, it was not until 1926 that American engineer Robert Goddard launched the first liquid fuel rocket using a mixture of liquid oxygen (to speed up the burning) and petrol.

▶▶ Read further › rockets
pg17 (f29)

▶ *In 1789, Herschel's telescope, which he built at his home in Bath, England, used mirrors that measured about 1.25 m across.*

▲ *Modern spacecraft use liquid oxygen and liquid hydrogen to fuel their engines.*

▶▶ Read further › solar / satellites
pg21 (j22); pg30 (k2)

The International Space Station will be more than 100 m in length and weigh over 400 tonnes

◄ Skylab, *30 m long, was launched into orbit by a Saturn V rocket in 1973. It disintegrated and fell from orbit in 1979.*

Read further › satellites
pg30 (k2)

Satellites

If you could look down on the Earth from outer space, you would not just see the Moon orbiting (moving round) the Earth but also lots of manufactured satellites. A satellite is any object that orbits a planet or a star. In 1957 the Russian satellite *Sputnik 1* was the first artificial satellite invented to orbit the Earth. Satellites carry out many tasks, from passing on television signals, telephone calls *(see pg27 [m22])* and e-mail messages, to recording the weather or helping ships or aeroplanes pinpoint their positions. Astronomers use satellites to learn about the universe.

Staying in space

In 1971 the Russians launched the first space station, called *Salyut*. It was a large spacecraft orbiting the Earth with room for people to live and work. Two years later, the first American space station, *Skylab*, went into orbit. *Skylab* had a workshop on the top floor and living quarters below. It was powered by solar panels. Experiments in space are carried out in conditions of low gravity. Materials such as electrical components are studied under conditions of no atmosphere and weightlessness. Astronauts perform experiments on themselves to see how humans could cope with living in space.

Read further › colonies
pg35 (b22)

◄ *The 'wings' of this satellite are the solar panels that contain photovoltaic cells. These cells turn the Sun's energy into electricity.*

INVENTIVE

• The first telescope was invented by a Dutch spectacle maker, Hans Lippershey, in 1608, but few people were interested.

• In 1610, Galileo invented the first true astronomical telescope, magnifying up to 30 times. This enabled him to observe Jupiter's four largest moons.

Probing the planets

Since the 1960s, unmanned spacecraft called space probes have been sent to explore the planets, moons, comets, asteroids and the Sun. Space probes are sophisticated robots that fly on a course pre-set by computers, sending back data to the Earth by radio. They can also send landing craft down to a planet's surface. In 1966 the Russian probe *Luna 9* landed on the Moon. Later the same year, the American probe *Surveyor 1* achieved the same. The *Viking* probes placed landers on Mars in 1976 and the twin *Voyager* space probes were sent to Jupiter, Saturn, Uranus and Neptune in 1977. In 1997 the Pathfinder mission landed the sojourner probe on Mars' surface.

▶ *The* Galileo *probe reached Jupiter in 1995, sending a smaller probe into Jupiter's atmosphere for a closer look.*

Check it out!
• http://spaceflight.nasa.gov

Read further › robots
pg34 (c33)

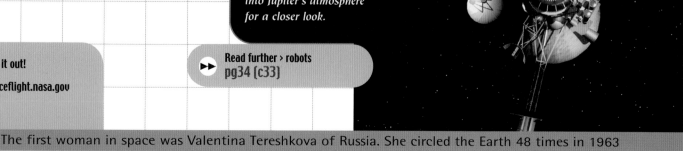

The first woman in space was Valentina Tereshkova of Russia. She circled the Earth 48 times in 1963

a b c d e f g h i j k l m n o p q r s t u v w

Into the future

ODAY THE pace of new technology moves very quickly, and we take for granted machines that have been invented recently. Future inventions could be more amazing than ever before. Virtual reality, flat-screen televisions and computer animation have changed the entertainment world. Robotic space explorers may pave the way for human exploration of other planets in the 21st century. Advances in gene therapy and cloning may have huge influences on the living world. Inventions, such as personal flying machines and ways to live at sea or on other planets could change our lives forever.

IT'S A FACT

• The first successful gene therapy – replacing faulty genes with new ones – took place on a four-year-old girl who was unable to fight infections.

• The first robot programed to respond to commands was an artificial duck created in 1738.

• In 2002, a South African millionaire paid $20 million for a 10-day 'holiday' in space.

House robots

The invention of the microchip in 1952 enabled the movement of machines, such as robots, to be controlled by computer. In the future, robots, such as this vacuum cleaner, may assist humans in many ways, such as doing the housework.

▼ *This robot vacuum cleaner contains sensors to stop it bumping into things or getting stuck in corners.*

Read further > robots
pg35 (c33)

▶ *The Solo Trek XFV is a compact aircraft with vertical take-off and landing. It has a potential 240-km range and a top speed of 129 km/h.*

Flying machine

In 2001, Michael Moshier and Robert Bulaga and their team invented a personal flying machine that straps on to a person's back: the Solo Trek XFV. On the test flight, Moshier hovered above the ground for only 19 seconds at an altitude of just 0.6 m, but this could indicate the start of a new method of flying.

Read further > flying / hovering
pg23 (b22; l22)

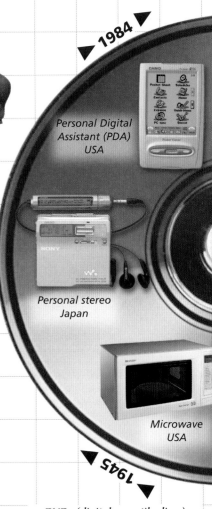

▲1984

Personal Digital Assistant (PDA) USA

1980

Personal stereo Japan

Microwave USA

▼1945

▲ *DVDs (digital versatile discs) store information such as music and films. DVD players use lasers to 'read' the information. DVDs are similar to CDs but they have the capacity to store much more information and have excellent sound and picture quality.*

In Britain, every month about 1000 new inventions are patented – the inventor is given rights and control over the idea

1 2 3 4 5 6 7 8 9 10 11 12 13 14 15 16 17 18 19

a b c d e f g h i j k l m n o p q r s t u v w

Living in space

Over the next couple of centuries, explorers may be able to set up colonies on Mars. Future NASA missions are planned to land Mars rovers and mobile laboratories with instruments for drilling below the surface, and detecting and analysing minerals and water samples. NASA is also developing technology to turn Martian resources into rocket fuel for the trip back.

▶▶ **Read further › space**
pg32 (d2)

▲ 1816 ▲

*Stethoscope
France*

▼ 1886 ▼

*Escalator
USA*

*Dishwasher
USA*

▲ 1907 ▲

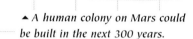
▲ *A human colony on Mars could be built in the next 300 years.*

INVENTIVE

• The HelpMate robot works in hospitals, delivering meals, letters and medicine.

• Instead of using PIN numbers, machines may identify people by their eyes or fingerprints.

▶▶ **Read further › sojourner**
pg33 (m29)

Intelligent robots

Robots have only been possible since computers were invented, which enabled robots to follow instructions. Robots were first patented in 1961 by American scientists George C. Devol and Joseph F. Engelberger. Today, thousands of robots go to places where people cannot go, such as the deep ocean or other planets. They do tedious and even dangerous jobs, such as handling hazardous, radioactive material. Robots have been used to explore the surface of other planets.

▼ *The robot* Sojourner *was a space probe sent onto the surface of Mars in 1997 to investigate the rock type.*

Floating city

The *Freedom* ship is planned to house up to 50,000 people. It claims to offer a solution to the problem of overcrowding on land. The ship is planned to contain a school, a hospital, yacht marinas, one of the largest shopping malls in the world, sports facilities, theatres, nightclubs, restaurants and a golf range.

▲ *The* Freedom *ship will recycle much of its waste, rather than dumping it into the ocean.*

▶▶ **Read further › recycling**
pg31 (i29)

 Check it out!

• http://www.newgadgets. freeserve.co.uk
• http://www.time.com/time/ 2001/inventions/
• http://www.wfs.org

James Dyson's bagless vacuum cleaner went through 5127 prototypes before it was ready to be manufactured

Glossary

Anaesthetic A substance that stops the body from feeling pain, sometimes making a person unconscious.

Animation Making drawings appear to move by using a series of very similar, but slightly different, drawings one after the other.

Antiseptic A substance that helps to prevent infection by stopping the growth of germs.

Astronaut A person trained to be a crew member in a spacecraft.

Astronomer A person who studies the stars, planets and other bodies in space.

Battery A device for storing electricity as chemical energy and changing it into electrical energy.

Cathode ray tube A tube inside many televisions, which makes the screen light up to form a picture.

Circuit A path around which an electric current flows.

Cloning Making an identical copy of an organism from one of its cells.

Compact disc (CD) A disc on which information, such as words, pictures, sound, computer games or computer software, can be stored as a series of bumps, which are 'read' by a laser beam.

Computer An electronic machine controlled by instructions called a program.

Condensation The process by which a gas turns into a liquid, such as air to water.

Contact lens A small lens worn in contact with the eye to correct vision.

Cuneiform Cuneiform writing was made by making wedge-shaped signs in soft clay.

Electric motor A device that changes electrical energy into movement.

Electron A particle with a negative charge that exists around the nucleus of an atom.

Electronics The use of electronic components to control the flow of current around a circuit.

E-mail (electronic mail) A way of sending messages over the Internet.

Endoscope A flexible tube with a special medical camera on the end, used to look inside patients' bodies.

Gears Wheels with teeth around the edge that fit together to change the speed or direction of movement.

Global warming The gradual warming of the Earth caused by pollution in the atmosphere, which traps the Earth's heat.

Hydro-electric power Electrical power generated by the force of falling water.

Industrial Revolution The rapid development of the use of machines in late 18th and early 19th century British industry.

Internal combustion engine An engine that uses a fuel, such as burning petrol mixed with air, to power a machine or vehicle.

Internet A vast computer network linking computers all over the world via satellites, optical fibres and telephone wires.

Irrigation Watering dry land to make it suitable for growing crops.

Laser A device that produces a thin, intensely bright, beam of light, that is one colour and one frequency.

Liquid crystal display (LCD) A display made with liquid crystals. A passing electric current lines them up, blocking the light and so forming patterns.

Microwave Radio waves with a short wavelength, which are used in cooking and telecommunications.

Ozone layer A layer of gas called ozone (a form of oxygen) high up in the Earth's atmosphere that absorbs most of the Sun's harmful ultraviolet radiation.

Patent The exclusive right to make, use or sell an invention for a set number of years. Inventors must apply for a patent.

Plough A device for cutting furrows in soil and turning it over, ready to sow new seeds.

Pollution The introduction into an environment of substances harmful to living things.

Radio waves Electromagnetic waves with the longest wavelength and lowest frequency, including microwaves and those used for radio and TV broadcasting.

Recycling Using the same materials, such as newspaper, over and over again.

Renewable resources Materials that can be used and replaced naturally, without being used up. The sun, wind and water are renewable energy resources.

Robot A machine that mimics the action of a human being.

Satellite Any object orbiting a star, planet or asteroid. Man-made satellites orbiting the Earth are used to gather scientific data or receive and transmit radio signals.

Solar cell A cell that converts the Sun's energy into electricity.

Space probe An unmanned spacecraft sent from Earth to investigate the Solar System and beyond.

Space station A spacecraft, big enough for people to live and work on, which orbits the Earth.

Spinning Drawing out and twisting fibres, such as wool or cotton, into threads to make yarn.

Vaccination Injecting a substance into the blood so that it produces antibodies, which provide protection against a disease

Index

The publishers would like to thank the following
artists who have contributed to this book:
Julie Banyard, Steve Cauldwell, Peter Dennis, Nick Farmer, Peter Gregory, Rob Jakeway, Janos Marffy,
Sebastian Quigley, Terry Riley, Peter Sarson, Mike Saunders, Rob Sheffield,
Roger Stewart, Mike White

The publishers wish to thank the following sources for the photographs used in this book:
Topham Picturepoint, p11 (b/l); Science Museum, London/HIP/Topham Picturepoint, p12 (c);
2000 Legoland A/S, p16 (m/r); Nissan, p22 (c); Sony, p24 (m/r); p34 (m/r);
Courtesy of Apple, p25 (m/l); Sony Computer Entertainment, p25 (t/r);
Nokia, p27 (b/r); Ford, p31 (m/l); Trek Aerospace, p34 (m);
Electrolux, p34 (b/l); Casio, p34 (m/r)

Cover photograph: **Frederic Sierakowski/Rex Features**

All other photographs are from:
Corel, digitalvision, Dover, Flat Earth, Hemera, ILN,
MKP Archives, PhotoDisc, STOCKbyte